DINOWORLD
Deinonychus

MICHAEL BENTON

Kingfisher

NEW YORK

CONTENTS

INTRODUCTION

Just when you thought that *Tyrannosaurus* was the most frightening dinosaur, *Deinonychus* rears its fearsome head. Unlike the gigantic tyrant king, however, *Deinonychus* was a small dinosaur, not much longer than 10 or 12 feet. Like other meat eaters, though, it had a mouth full of sharp, pointed teeth for cutting into flesh. Add to that, the sharp claws at the ends of the fingers and you have a formidable predator. But what made this dinosaur much more frightening than any other meat eater of its time was the huge savage claw on the second toe of each foot. In fact, *Deinonychus* was given its name (meaning "terrible claw") because of the whopping big can openers on its toes! With great agility, *Deinonychus* would bound after its prey, striking at it with its razor-sharp hind feet, and then ripping and tearing until the animal was dead.

To make matters worse, *Deinonychus* was quite intelligent by dinosaur standards. Probably hunting in packs, these animals may have used their intelligence to track their prey, working out the best time to make their move. When these deadly hunters were around, there wasn't much chance for any other dinosaur that *Deinonychus* chose to chase.

Where did all this information and these ideas about *Deinonychus* come from? None of it had even been guessed at 30 years ago, when this important dinosaur was discovered. It took dinosaur hunter John Ostrom and other scientists to piece together the puzzle of the sickle-clawed dinosaur. His discoveries in the wilds of Wyoming and Montana made scientists realize that dinosaurs were far from being slow and dim-witted failures, but rather the most active and clever successes of their times! The discovery of *Deinonychus* also made people realize that while *Tyrannosaurus* may have been the largest meat eater of all time, *Deinonychus* has got to be the scariest! The pages that follow show how we came to learn all this — and more — about the Terrible Claw.

David B. Weishampel
Associate Professor
Johns Hopkins University

A DINOSAUR TIMELINE

Dinosaurs lived on Earth for about 165 million years. But *Deinonychus* was only around for part of the Dinosaur Age — sometime during the 50-million-year interval called the early Cretaceous. This was an important time in dinosaur evolution. Earlier periods had been dominated by giant plant-eating dinosaurs such as *Brachiosaurus*. But by the early Cretaceous, the chief plant eaters were two-legged dinosaurs such as *Iguanodon*. Other species included meat eaters such as *Baryonyx*, as well as armored, plant-eating dinosaurs such as *Sauropelta*.

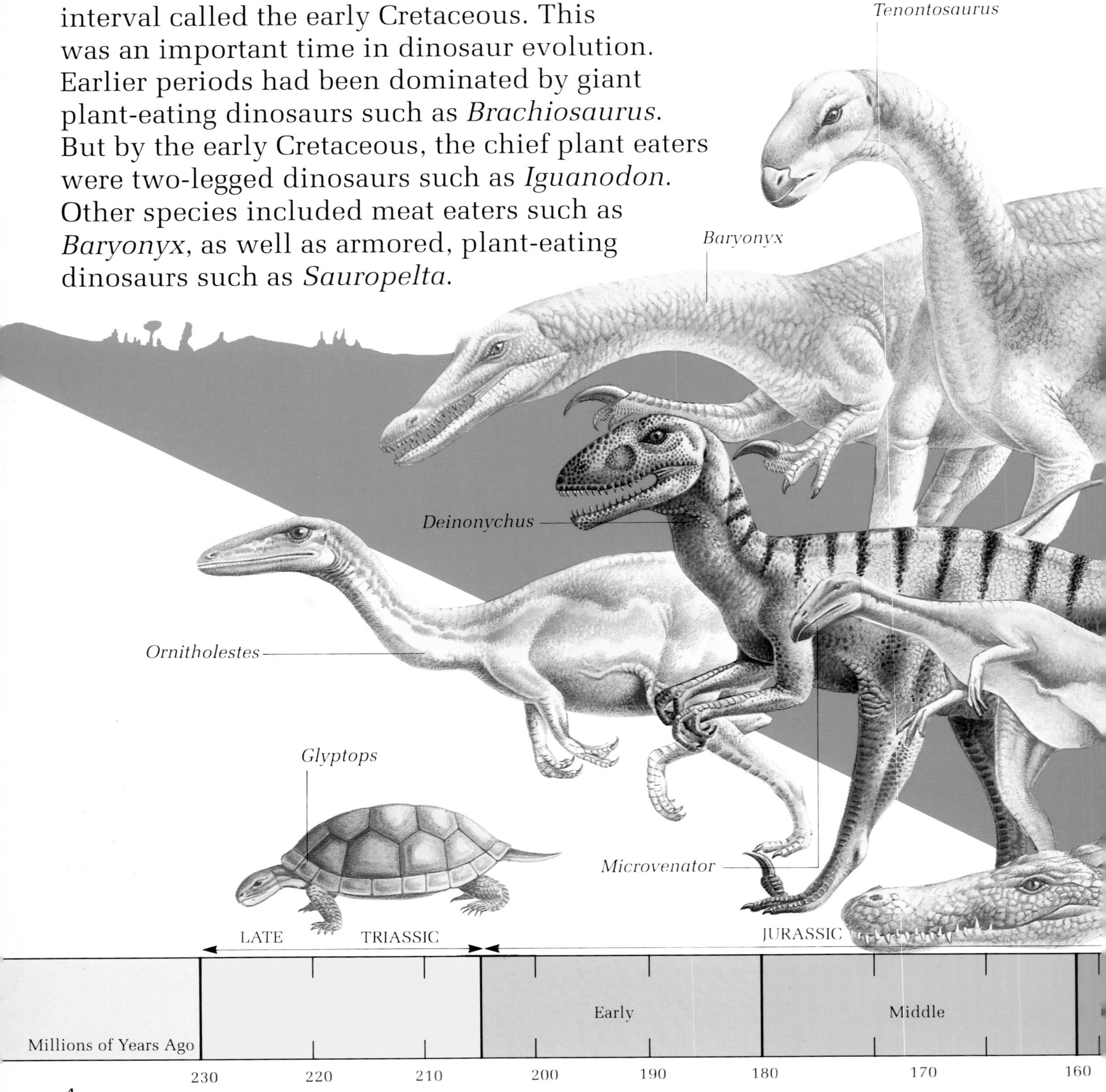

Tenontosaurus

Baryonyx

Deinonychus

Ornitholestes

Glyptops

Microvenator

	LATE	TRIASSIC		JURASSIC		
				Early		Middle
Millions of Years Ago						
230	220	210	200	190	180	170	160

Pterodactylus

Iguanodon

▼ Typical early Cretaceous dinosaurs included the meat eaters *Deinonychus* and *Baryonyx*. Although different in many ways, they both had big slashing claws. Two-legged plant eaters included *Iguanodon* and *Hypsilophodon*, a close relative of *Tenontosaurus*, a prey of *Deinonychus*. There were also ankylosaurs, such as *Sauropelta*, as well as turtles, pterosaurs, and crocodiles.

Hypsilophodon

Sauropelta

Goniopholis

▼ Life on Earth is measured in millions of years, divided up into units. Dinosaurs lived during the Mesozoic era, which is divided into three periods, the Triassic, Jurassic, and Cretaceous. Dinosaurs lived from the late Triassic to the end of the Cretaceous.

CRETACEOUS

Early	Late

145   130   120   110   100   95   90   80   70   65

110 MILLION YEARS AGO

When *Deinonychus* was alive, a map of the world looked quite different from a map of today's world. This is because the continents and oceans have been moving slowly sideways for millions of years. At that time, the world had a tropical climate, with plenty of rain. As it was warm as far north and as far south as the polar regions, dinosaurs had a wider range than modern reptiles.

▼ In Cretaceous times there was only a bit of the Atlantic Ocean between North America and Africa. The coastlines of parts of present-day America and Europe were covered by seas. The probable position of some mountain ranges are shown on the map.

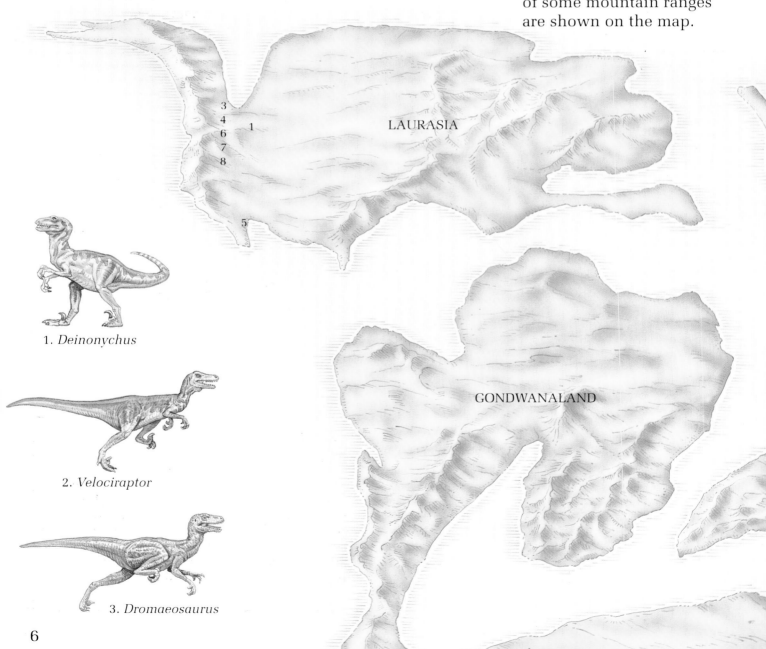

LAURASIA

GONDWANALAND

1. *Deinonychus*

2. *Velociraptor*

3. *Dromaeosaurus*

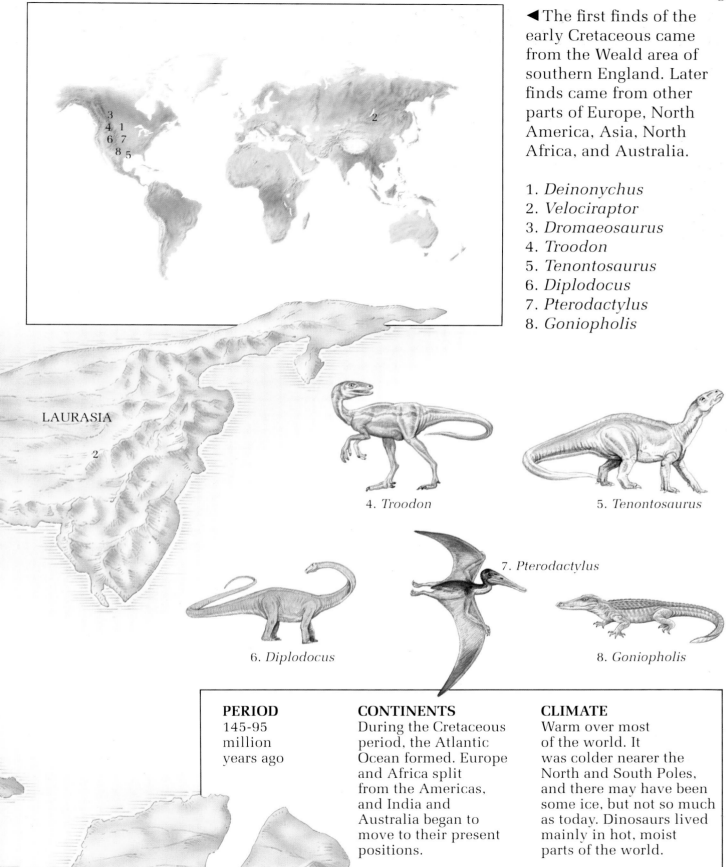

◄ The first finds of the early Cretaceous came from the Weald area of southern England. Later finds came from other parts of Europe, North America, Asia, North Africa, and Australia.

1. *Deinonychus*
2. *Velociraptor*
3. *Dromaeosaurus*
4. *Troodon*
5. *Tenontosaurus*
6. *Diplodocus*
7. *Pterodactylus*
8. *Goniopholis*

LAURASIA

4. *Troodon*

5. *Tenontosaurus*

6. *Diplodocus*

7. *Pterodactylus*

8. *Goniopholis*

PERIOD
145-95 million years ago

CONTINENTS
During the Cretaceous period, the Atlantic Ocean formed. Europe and Africa split from the Americas, and India and Australia began to move to their present positions.

CLIMATE
Warm over most of the world. It was colder nearer the North and South Poles, and there may have been some ice, but not so much as today. Dinosaurs lived mainly in hot, moist parts of the world.

THE MONTANA BADLANDS

Deinonychus's world was quite different from present-day Montana, where its remains were found. About 110 million years ago, this semidesert was subtropical lowland. Cycads, ferns, and horsetails supplied food for plant-eating dinosaurs. Dragonflies and other insects flew over pools, which were full of fish and snails.

▶ The cannonball-like cycads, and the ferns and horsetails, were all larger, more primitive versions of modern plants.

▶ Dragonflies are some of the most primitive insects. They have two pairs of wings that flap with different timing. Some of the prehistoric dragonflies were very large.

▶ A plant-eating *Tenontosaurus* watches the pack of *Deinonychus* chasing one of its herd.

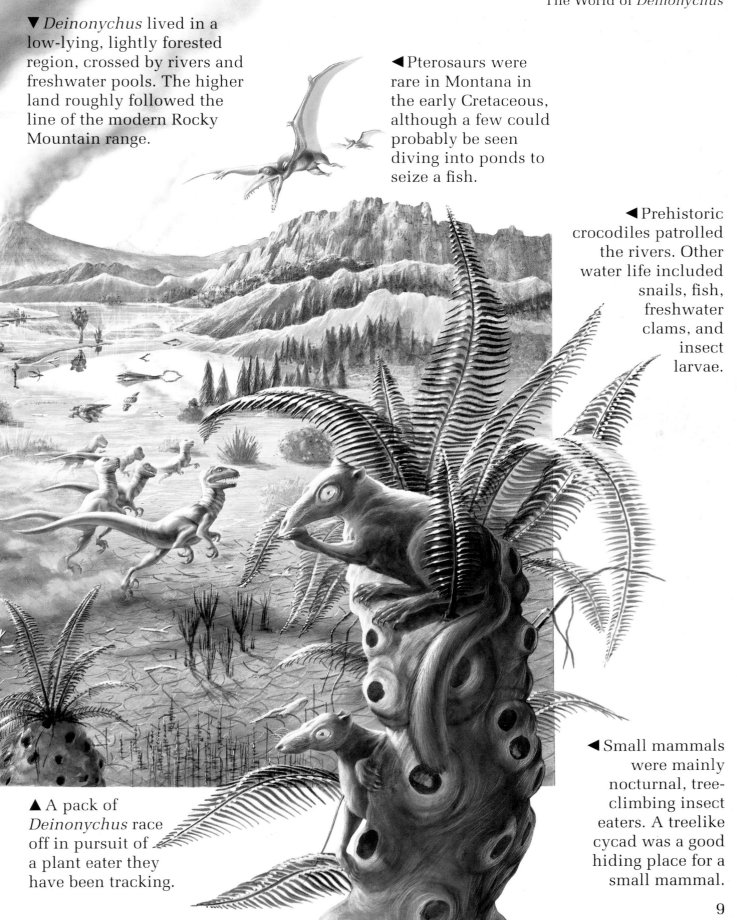

▼ *Deinonychus* lived in a low-lying, lightly forested region, crossed by rivers and freshwater pools. The higher land roughly followed the line of the modern Rocky Mountain range.

◄Pterosaurs were rare in Montana in the early Cretaceous, although a few could probably be seen diving into ponds to seize a fish.

◄Prehistoric crocodiles patrolled the rivers. Other water life included snails, fish, freshwater clams, and insect larvae.

◄Small mammals were mainly nocturnal, tree-climbing insect eaters. A treelike cycad was a good hiding place for a small mammal.

▲ A pack of *Deinonychus* race off in pursuit of a plant eater they have been tracking.

ANIMALS OF THE BADLANDS

It is fun to work out what dinosaurs ate. It is also fun to work out what ate dinosaurs. It seems likely that *Deinonychus* had no real enemies, as no giant meat eaters have been found in Montana. However, many other plants and animals lived on the land, and in the ponds and lakes. These may give clues about some of the things that *Deinonychus* ate. Fossil bones of fish, turtles, and crocodiles have been found with *Deinonychus*, while plants, shells, insects, pterosaurs, and early mammals have been found in nearby rocks of the same age.

Land Plants

When *Deinonychus* lived, the tallest trees were conifers, trees similar to modern pines and firs. There may have been a few flowers, but there was no grass.

Early Mammals

Mammals were the size of rats or mice; they fed mainly on insects.

Crocodiles

Goniopholis, a large crocodile, is munching a flat-shelled turtle, like a bony hamburger.

Turtles

The large freshwater turtle *Glytops* probably lived in ponds, where it hunted small fish.

Water beetle

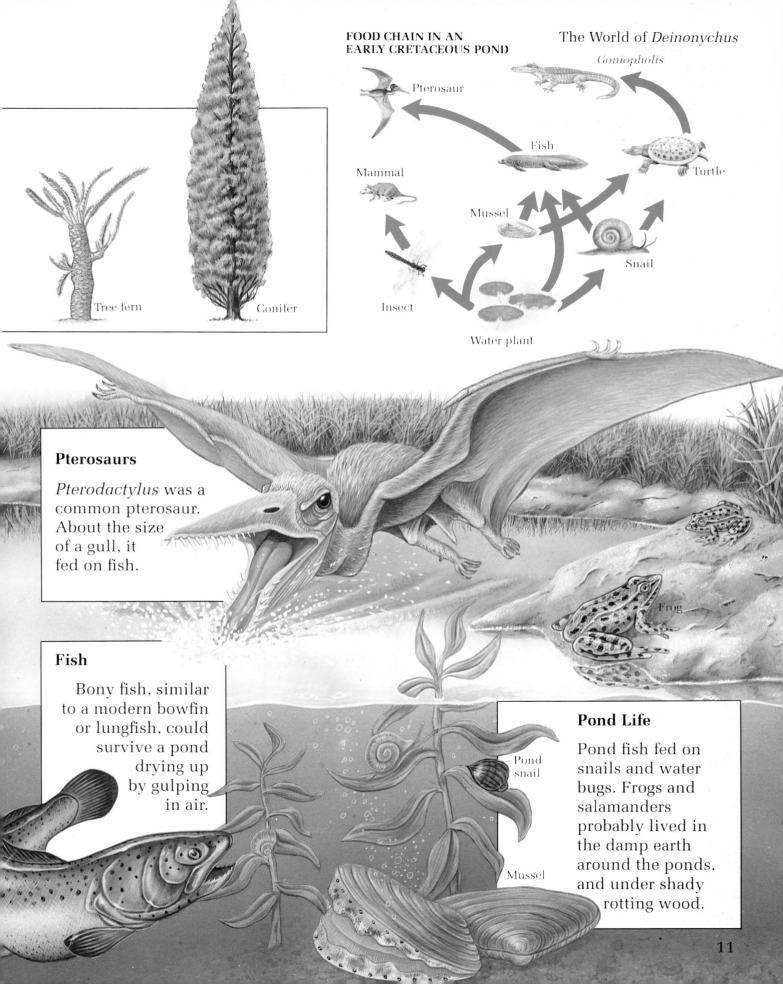

Tree fern

Conifer

FOOD CHAIN IN AN EARLY CRETACEOUS POND

The World of *Deinonychus*

Goniopholis

Pterosaur

Fish

Turtle

Mammal

Mussel

Snail

Insect

Water plant

Pterosaurs

Pterodactylus was a common pterosaur. About the size of a gull, it fed on fish.

Frog

Fish

Bony fish, similar to a modern bowfin or lungfish, could survive a pond drying up by gulping in air.

Pond snail

Mussel

Pond Life

Pond fish fed on snails and water bugs. Frogs and salamanders probably lived in the damp earth around the ponds, and under shady rotting wood.

PREY

Although *Deinonychus* was not large, it was capable of attacking any other early Cretaceous dinosaur. Even bigger dinosaurs, such as the plant eater *Tenontosaurus*, was part of *Deinonychus*'s diet. *Tenontosaurus* was the most common dinosaur in Montana in early Cretaceous times. Its neighbors included the giant sauropod *Diplodocus*, and the armored ankylosaur *Sauropelta*. There were also some smaller meat-eating dinosaurs, living side-by-side with *Deinonychus*, that may have stolen eggs and baby dinosaurs from the nests of the plant eaters.

▼ The mother dinosaur laid up to 20 eggs in a shallow nest. After the babies had hatched, adults brought them leaves until they could feed themselves. The parents had to keep watch because small meat eaters were often waiting to snatch their helpless babies!

Microvenator
MIKE-roe-ven-AH-tor
"SMALL HUNTER"
4 FT. (1.2 M) LONG

Microvenator was a sneaky little dinosaur that may have robbed nests.

Tenontosaurus

Ten-ONT-oh-SAW-rus
"SINEW REPTILE"
15-21 FT. (4.5-6.5 M) LONG

It is likely that these gigantic plant eaters moved around together in search of food. This helped to protect them from attack.

Sauropelta

SAW-roh-PEL-ta
"SHIELDED REPTILE"
20 FT. (7 M) LONG

A heavily armored dinosaur that belonged to the nodosaurid family of ankylosaurs.

Diplodocus

Dip-LOD-oh-kus
"DOUBLE BEAM"
100 FT. (30 M) LONG

This four-legged plant eater had an amazingly long neck and tail.

THE KILLER CLAW

Deinonychus was a terrifying killing machine whose body was designed for maximum speed and agility. Besides being able to run very fast, it also had a complete range of body weapons. It had a strong, lightly built skull, with tearing teeth. It also had a razor-sharp claw on each finger and toe. But its greatest weapon was the scythelike, 5-inch (12-centimeter)-long, "terrible claw" on the second toe of its back foot. This huge claw had a large bony core, which would have been covered by an even longer horny talon. When *Deinonychus* walked, it held the slashing claw up in a resting position. Some people have suggested that *Deinonychus* might have had feathers, but this is unlikely.

Deinonychus

DIE-no-NIKE-US
"TERRIBLE CLAW"
12 FT. (4 M) LONG

The nearly complete fossil of this agile predator was one of the most exciting dinosaur discoveries of the 1960s.

ARC OF "TERRIBLE CLAW"

Bony rods to hold tail straight

DEINONYCHUS FOOT AND CLAW

Foot

Claw in resting position

Toe

◄ When *Deinonychus* attacked, it raised its foot, as it leaped through the air. It then swung its back leg down, while bringing its claw over faster than the eye could see. It was capable of ripping a yard-long wound in the side of its victim.

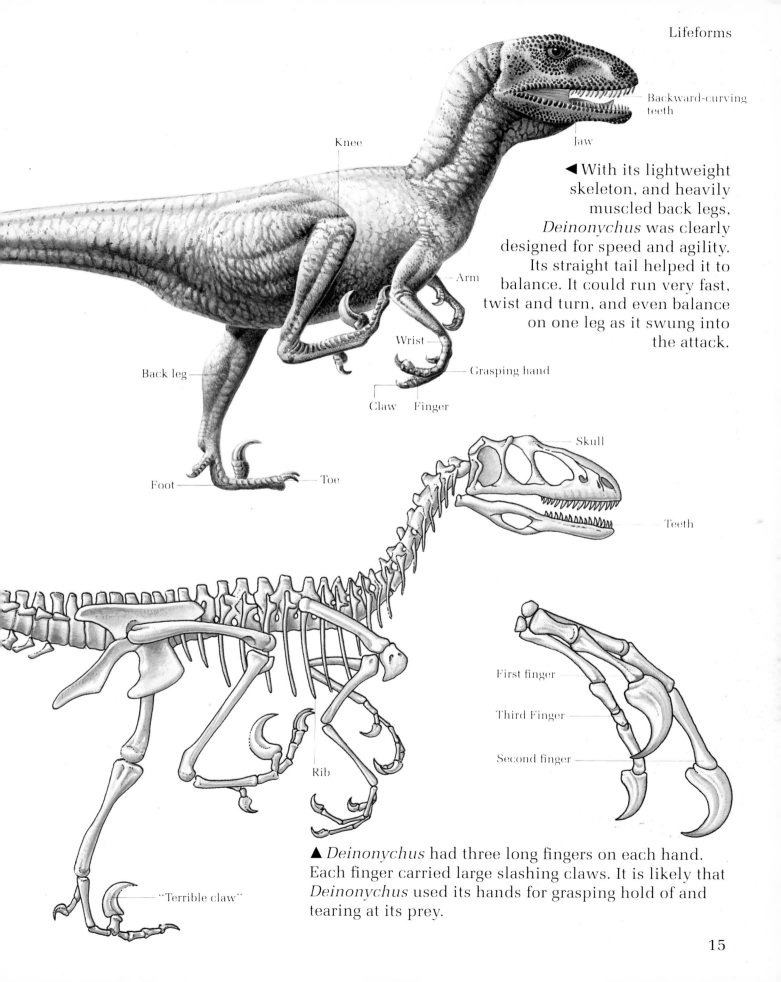

Knee

Backward-curving
teeth

Jaw

◄ With its lightweight
skeleton, and heavily
muscled back legs,
Deinonychus was clearly
designed for speed and agility.
Its straight tail helped it to
balance. It could run very fast,
twist and turn, and even balance
on one leg as it swung into
the attack.

Arm

Wrist

Grasping hand

Back leg

Claw   Finger

Foot

Toe

Skull

Teeth

First finger

Third Finger

Second finger

Rib

"Terrible claw"

▲ *Deinonychus* had three long fingers on each hand.
Each finger carried large slashing claws. It is likely that
Deinonychus used its hands for grasping hold of and
tearing at its prey.

15

KILLER INSTINCTS

Dinosaurs were usually not very clever, but *Deinonychus* may have been an exception. Because of the speed with which it attacked its prey, *Deinonychus* had to be able to think quickly. Its big brain also indicates exceptionally good eyesight. Like its relation *Troodon*, *Deinonychus* may also have had forward-facing eyes. Most dinosaurs were like the majority of modern animals, and saw a different scene with each eye. That is why a horse or a duck shakes its head from side to side when it comes up to you.

◀ When *Deinonychus* attacked, it balanced on one leg, moved forward, turned rapidly, and swung down with its claw.

▼ *Deinonychus* probably had a top speed of about 20 miles (35 km) an hour. This is about the same as the top speed of an ostrich or a racehorse.

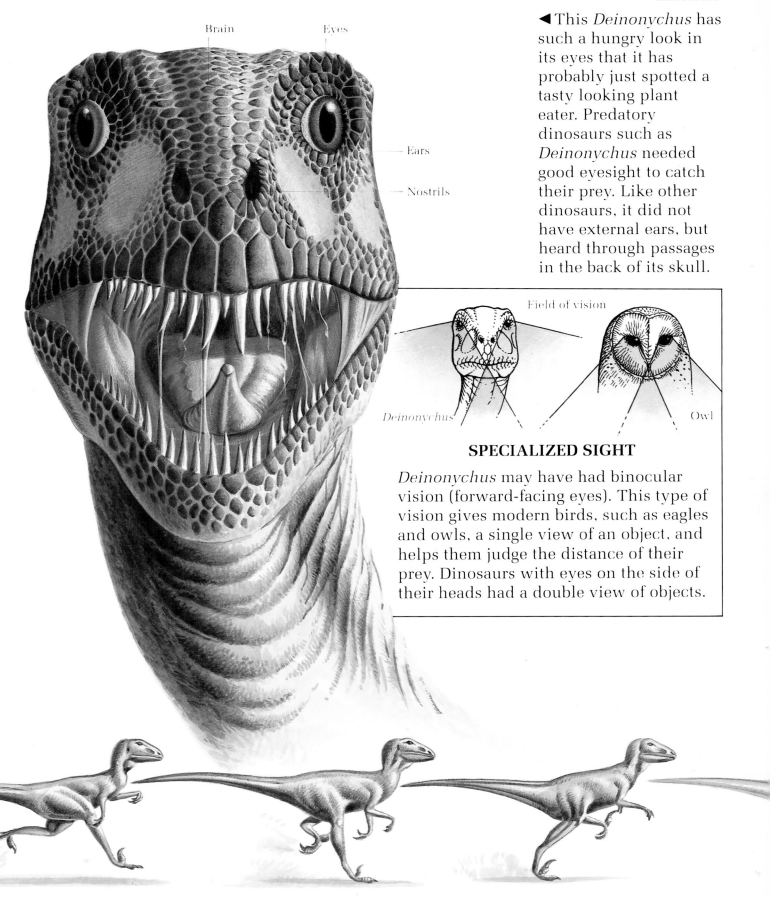

Brain   Eyes

Ears

Nostrils

◀ This *Deinonychus* has
such a hungry look in
its eyes that it has
probably just spotted a
tasty looking plant
eater. Predatory
dinosaurs such as
Deinonychus needed
good eyesight to catch
their prey. Like other
dinosaurs, it did not
have external ears, but
heard through passages
in the back of its skull.

Field of vision

Deinonychus   Owl

SPECIALIZED SIGHT

Deinonychus may have had binocular
vision (forward-facing eyes). This type of
vision gives modern birds, such as eagles
and owls, a single view of an object, and
helps them judge the distance of their
prey. Dinosaurs with eyes on the side of
their heads had a double view of objects.

PACK AND ATTACK

A big game hunter, *Deinonychus* was probably also a top team player. The prey of this dinosaur almost certainly included larger dinosaurs, such as *Tenontosaurus*, and giants such as *Diplodocus*. It is possible that *Deinonychus* only ate smaller dinosaurs. It may also have hunted alone, as some big cats do, killing a larger animal by biting or slashing at its neck. However, it is more likely that *Deinonychus* was clever enough to work out a game plan of hunting in swift-moving killer packs.

▼ *Deinonychus*'s favorite meal was probably *Tenontosaurus*. However, as *Tenontosaurus* was six times larger than its attackers, it would have taken four or five *Deinonychus* to kill one of these monsters. The pack's plan would have been to leap at its prey, and slash *Tenontosaurus*'s sides with their claws.

▼ With their body armor of bony back plates and spines, the ankylosaurs could usually protect themselves from attack. A further defensive measure was for an ankylosaur to crouch close to the ground, like a turtle. However, if two or three *Deinonychus* pulled an ankylosaur such as *Sauropelta* onto its back, they could then slash at its unprotected underside.

PACK ANIMALS

Hunting dogs and wolves are modern animals that hunt in packs. Each pack has a leader, and everyone in the pack has a job to do. The pack selects a victim and separates it from the rest of the herd. It then chases the victim, until it is exhausted, and can be dragged down and killed.

▶ Because of their size, *Deinonychus* would have found fully grown sauropods, such as *Diplodocus*, the most difficult prey to kill. In the picture, the killer pack has chosen to attack a young *Diplodocus* that has become separated from its family group. Four *Deinonychus* are about to close in on the doomed youngster.

A FAMILY CIRCLE

Deinonychus was a member of a fearsome group of meat-eating dinosaurs called the Deinonychosauria. The dinosaurs in this group are easily recognized by the large slashing claw on the second toe of each foot. There were at least two deinonychosaur families. The Dromaeosauridae includes medium-sized predators such as *Deinonychus*, *Dromaeosaurus*, and *Velociraptor*. The Saurornithoididae includes lightly built predators such as *Troodon*, and possibly larger dinosaurs, such as *Deinocheirus*.

▲ So far, the only parts of *Deinocheirus* that have been found are its amazing arms. Until more bones are found, we can only guess that the arms belonged to a giant flesh eater.

Dromaeosaurus
DROME-ee-oh-SAW-rus
"RUNNING REPTILE"
6 FT. (1.8 M) LONG

Troodon
Tro-o-don
"WOUNDING TOOTH"
6 FT. (2 M) LONG

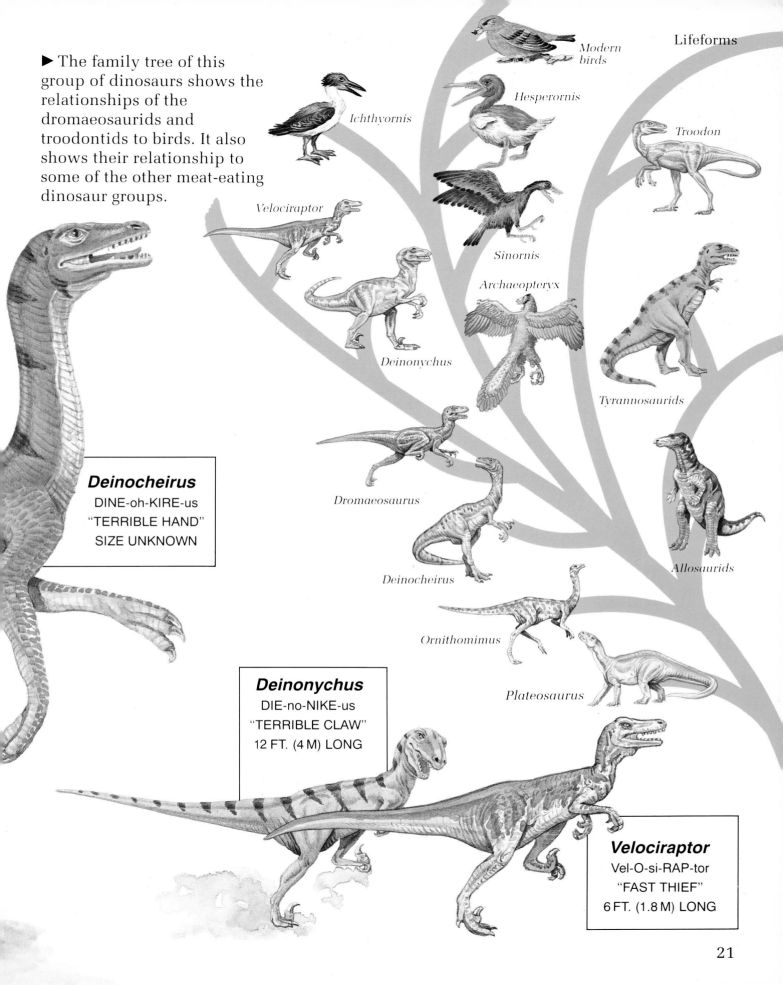

► The family tree of this group of dinosaurs shows the relationships of the dromaeosaurids and troodontids to birds. It also shows their relationship to some of the other meat-eating dinosaur groups.

Modern birds

Ichthyornis

Hesperornis

Troodon

Velociraptor

Sinornis

Archaeopteryx

Deinonychus

Tyrannosaurids

Dromaeosaurus

Deinocheirus

Allosaurids

Ornithomimus

Plateosaurus

Deinocheirus
DINE-oh-KIRE-us
"TERRIBLE HAND"
SIZE UNKNOWN

Deinonychus
DIE-no-NIKE-us
"TERRIBLE CLAW"
12 FT. (4 M) LONG

Velociraptor
Vel-O-si-RAP-tor
"FAST THIEF"
6 FT. (1.8 M) LONG

A DEADLY CONTEST

In 1971, a remarkable fossil of two dinosaurs fighting was dug up in Mongolia. A *Velociraptor* was caught fighting a *Protoceratops*, a small plant-eating horned dinosaur. *Protoceratops* was one of the first horned dinosaurs, a group that later included the giant *Triceratops*. In early Cretaceous Mongolia, large numbers of *Protoceratops* fed on the tough low plants. In the 1920s, a number of *Protoceratops* nests were dug up and fossil babies were found. Perhaps this *Velociraptor* was trying to rob the *Protoceratops* nest, and the mother or father came to fight off the attacker.

▼ Although it was more lightly built than *Deinonychus*, *Velociraptor* was just as deadly. However, on at least one occasion, it was obviously not strong enough to overcome a heavily armored plant eater, such as *Protoceratops*.

Protoceratops
Pro-toe-SER-a-tops
"FIRST HORNED FACE"
6 FT. (1.8 M) LONG

Protoceratops had no horns but a pointed beak and a head shield.

▼ The fossil remains of two dinosaurs locked in combat. *Velociraptor* seems to be gripping the head shield of *Protoceratops*, while lashing with its giant claw. At the same time, *Protoceratops* has pierced *Velociraptor*'s chest.

DEINONYCHUS AND BIRDS

Birds are living dinosaurs. When the first fossil of *Archaeopteryx* was found in Germany, in 1861, it appeared to be a reptile skeleton with a bird's feathers. Amazingly, the prints of the feathers were to be seen in the limestone around the bones. These feathers were very like those of living birds. Here was a "missing link" between reptiles and birds! It has now been proved that *Deinonychus* is one of the closest dinosaur relatives of birds.

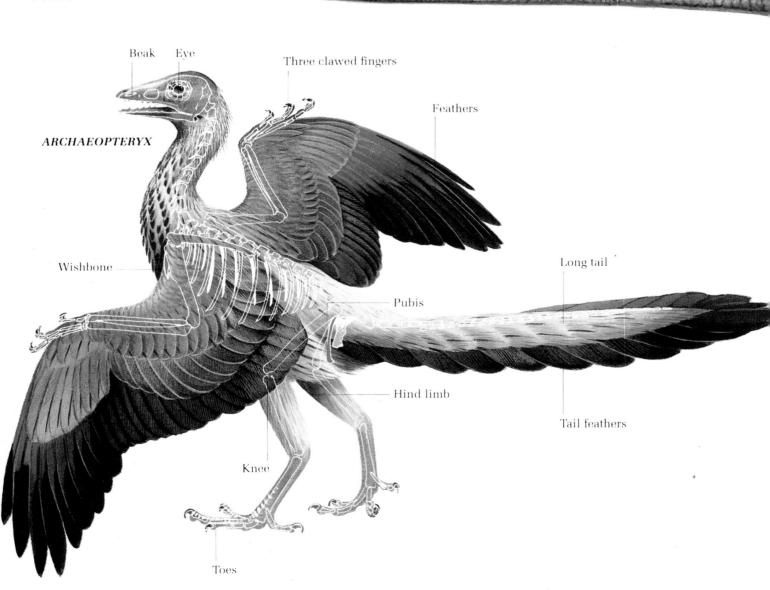

Long tail

ARCHAEOPTERYX

Beak

Eye

Three clawed fingers

Feathers

Wishbone

Pubis

Long tail

Hind limb

Tail feathers

Knee

Toes

DEINONYCHUS

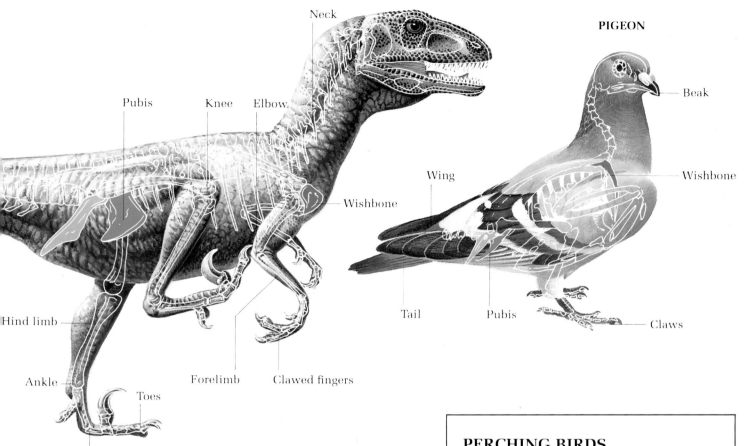

Neck

Pubis Knee Elbow

Wishbone

Hind limb

Ankle

Toes

Forelimb Clawed fingers

Foot

PIGEON

Beak

Wing

Wishbone

Tail Pubis

Claws

▲ *Deinonychus* is very like the early birds. Its light skull and short backward-curved teeth are nearly the same. The three-toed feet are also the same, although birds do not have a slashing claw. *Archaeopteryx*, the first bird, is really a dinosaur with feathers. It has a long bony tail, three fingers on its hand, a long thin neck, and a lightly built skull with teeth in its jaws. Modern birds have lost their teeth and their bony tails. The tail is now just a short stump of bones which support the tail feathers. Also, the fingers on the wing have become much smaller, and they do not have claws any longer. Finally, birds today have a breast bone to support the powerful wing muscles.

PERCHING BIRDS

If the first bird was *Archaeopteryx*, the last, and most successful, birds to evolve were the perching birds. Perching birds evolved about 25 million years ago. About half of all modern birds belong to this group.

Swallows are perching birds.

EARLY FLYING MACHINES

How could a land-living dinosaur become a flying bird? Did some dinosaurs take to the trees and jump from branch to branch? Or did flying evolve as a way of helping small dinosaurs to leap after insect prey? Indeed, could the early birds like *Archaeopteryx* actually fly, or did they just glide gently from tree to tree? All of these questions are being debated by scientists. Some scientists have even questioned whether *Archaeopteryx* had feathers: they have suggested that the feathers seen in fossils were faked. It seems, however, that the feathers are genuine; they are beautifully preserved in the limestone around the bones. This limestone is so unusual that many other soft-bodied fossils have been found in it, including worms, fish, and other animals.

Flightless bird's feather

Quill

Archaeopteryx feather

▲ In flying birds, the quill is set to one side. In flightless birds, the quill runs up the middle. So *Archaeopteryx* was a flyer.

▲ One theory about how birds learned to fly is that they first flew **from the ground up**. The prebird dinosaurs may have used their feathered arms to help them leap in the air when catching insects.

► Another theory, is that flying began **from the trees down**. Prebird dinosaurs would glide down from trees to catch insects. Over time, the prebirds would have glided farther, until they became fully flying birds.

Hoatzin chick

A THROWBACK

Do any living birds give clues about the first birds? Baby hoatzins have tiny claws on their wings. They live near rivers in northern South America. Their claws are a throwback to the first birds. The claws don't appear in adult hoatzins.

DINOFACTS

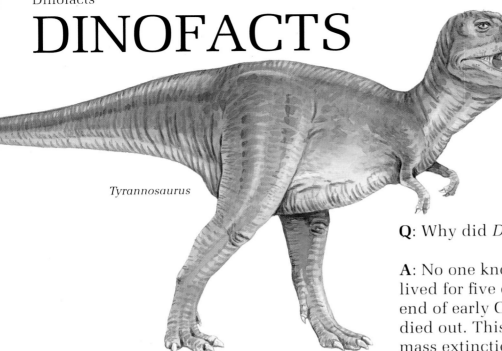

Tyrannosaurus

Deinonychus

Q: Was *Deinonychus* the most dangerous dinosaur that ever lived?

A: *Deinonychus* was the most dangerous small dinosaur. It was shorter than an adult human being, but it could run faster. It would have been able to kill even the strongest man with its terrifying claw. There were other, bigger, meat eaters though. *Tyrannosaurus* was the biggest of all. Forty feet (12 m) long and 20 feet (6 m) high: its mouth opened so wide that a child could have stood up inside (before being swallowed)!

Q: Why did *Deinonychus* die out?

A: No one knows. Probably *Deinonychus* lived for five or ten million years, near the end of early Cretaceous times, and then died out. This was long before the famous mass extinction of the dinosaurs, which happened 40 million years later. Possibly, *Deinonychus* disappeared because the animals it fed on, such as *Tenontosaurus*, died out. Or perhaps local climates, in what is now Montana, changed in some way so that this dinosaur could no longer survive.

Q: What noises did *Deinonychus* make?

A: Modern reptiles, such as snakes, can hiss. However, living reptiles cannot sing, since they do not have voice boxes in their throats. Maybe, though, *Deinonychus* was able to sing like its close relatives, the birds. No one knows whether the first birds could sing. But if they could, possibly *Deinonychus* could sing as well. The songs would have been pretty terrible though; screeches and squawks like a rusty old bicycle.

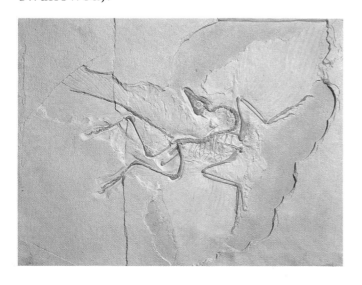

A fossil of *Archaeopteryx*, the first bird

Q: Will scientists ever make a living *Velociraptor*, as is shown in the film *Jurassic Park*?

Velociraptor

Newly hatched *Deinonychus* young

Q: How did *Deinonychus* breed, and what were its babies like?

A: So far nobody has found either the eggs or babies of *Deinonychus*. However, all dinosaurs laid eggs, just as birds and most reptiles do today. Probably the eggs were laid in an earth nest on the ground, and then covered with leaves to keep them warm. The babies were probably very small when they hatched. They would have been fierce little monsters that would have snapped and torn at your fingers. The parents would have fed them with lizards and insects, until they were big enough to hunt for themselves.

Q: Did *Deinonychus* have any large relatives?

A: *Deinonychus* and *Velociraptor* were about the height of eight- or ten-year-old children. But a bigger relative, called informally "*Utahraptor*," has been reported. It is based on a single, sicklelike slashing claw, found in Utah in 1993. So far, all we know is that the claw came from the foot of a dinosaur belonging to the same group as *Deinonychus* (the dromaeosaurs), and that the rocks it was found in were of an earlier period than the Cretaceous.

A: Scientists will not be able to build a whole dinosaur for a long time, if ever. The basis of the film is factual: dinosaur cells have been studied for a long time. Recently, dinosaur proteins have been purified in the laboratory. Also, there are many examples of insects that lived in the "Age of the Dinosaurs" that have been preserved in amber (fossil resin), and many of their proteins are still there. The problem is to take these bits of protein and clone them (make them grow) in some way that would ever give you a single cell, let alone a complete living breathing animal. However, who knows what might happen in 50 years time!

Prehistoric insects trapped in amber

FINDING *DEINONYCHUS*

Deinonychus was one of the most exciting recent dinosaur discoveries. In 1964, Professor John Ostrom, and his assistant, Grant Meyer, were out prospecting for dinosaur bones in the Montana Badlands. In the side of a great rounded butte, the two paleontologists spotted some human-sized finger bones. They excitedly brushed away the dirt, and found an extraordinary long three-fingered hand, each finger ending in a fearsome claw. They realized they had found a remarkable new kind of flesh-eating dinosaur.

▲ Professor John Ostrom, pictured shortly after he found *Deinonychus* in 1964.

▶ The first find of *Deinonychus* was two large sharp claws. After careful brushing and scraping away, the rock and dirt were removed to reveal a three-fingered grasping hand.

▼ The *Deinonychus* dig site is located low in a hillside, near the town of Billings, Montana. The 200-foot (60 m)-high butte is made from layers of multicolored sands and muds laid down in ancient rivers and lakes. After Ostrom discovered the foot and hand, he found many more *Deinonychus* bones nearby. It then took him years of careful work in the laboratory before he could reconstruct a skeleton.

Ominous Mound, Montana

Dig site

► *Deinonychus*'s foot was the second part of the skeleton to be found by Ostrom and Meyer. After careful brushing and cleaning, the foot turned out to be complete, and perfectly preserved. The huge claw on the foot gave *Deinonychus* its name of "terrible claw."

DINOVENTURES
AMBUSH!

All known facts about dinosaurs and their habitats have been entered into a computer program called DINO, designed by world-famous paleontologist Dr. Karl Harlow. He has linked this up to a Virtual Reality machine with controls that allow the operators to move through the computer generated landscapes, as though they are living dinosaurs themselves. Dr. Harlow has devised a number of "games" that will allow him to observe how dinosaurs may have behaved under certain circumstances. To this he has added the "Random Effect" — unpredictable consequences caused by the presence of the player in the game. The players are his children: Buddy, a thirteen-year-old girl who is brilliant at computer games, and Rob, her ten-year-old brother, who is mad about dinosaurs and wants to be a paleontologist. When "playing" DINO, Buddy and Rob will have to get as close to the "virtual" dinosaurs as possible. They may even have to kill to survive, or become hunted themselves and risk "death by dinosaur!"

The Virtual
Reality helmet

Buddy clipped on the Virtual Reality helmet with practiced ease. She and Rob had flipped a coin to see who would play DINO first and she had won. Her father had already warned her that the graphics would be alarmingly realistic. He had insisted on a pulse monitor, to ensure that if she became too frightened he could close down the system. It was therefore with a mixture of excitement and dread that she entered this Virtual world. Her eyes adjusted to the screen saver

— pteranodons sailing across a bright blue backdrop. Her father's voice spoke to her from a point midway between her ears:

"OK, Buddy? Can you hear me?"

"Loud and clear Dad," she said, and made herself comfortable in the VR harness. The VR screen could take a person through 360 degrees with sickening speed. The controls in the glove and the helmet were ultrasensitive. She changed the screen with a small movement of her thumb.

"You know what you have to do, Buddy," her father continued. "You are about to enter Dinoworld to observe the Deinonychosaurs and the program has selected *Microvenator* as your biovehicle. You can get the comparison on your screen with the Dinodata icon." Biovehicle was the strange name for the dinosaur identity that she would have for the duration of the game. Her view of everything would be set at its eye level, her speed its speed, its teeth and claws would be her teeth and claws, and its enemies and predators would be hers,too.

"The Deinonychosaurs have been given an intelligence rating of 5, but the Random Effect may have increased this, so be careful. One more thing," Dr. Harlow said, "Good luck."

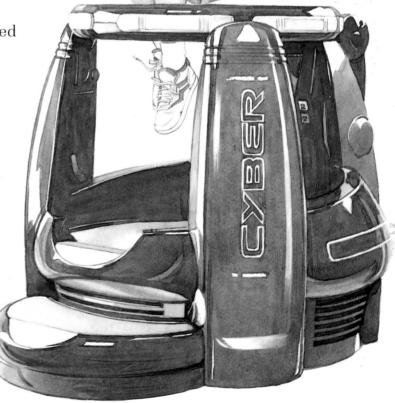

The screen saver dissolved and was replaced with a lakeside scene in early dawn light. There were palm trees but no flowers or grasses anywhere in the Cretaceous landscape. Buddy went through the orientation procedure, choosing with her Virtual "hand" from the onscreen menus. She chose RECORD and began her verbal report.

"I've arrived — I think. The year counter reads 115 MY and the clock 6:23 A.M. I'm by a lake somewhere ... let's see. I'm trying the locator. Right.

"Iowa — 50 miles west of modern Des Moines. Terrain is flat, sandy to pebbly, and vegetation is mostly scrub with areas of dense ferns. Cover for *Microvenator* is fair to good, but there are tar pit hazards. Choosing DINODATA.

"Seems there's a herd of *Tenontosaurus* 4 miles west, moving south east; solitary *Ornithomimus* 2 miles north of here, moving south along the lakeside — I'll have to keep a look out for him. Bingo! Five Deinons 2 miles due east, moving this way. They are probably coming to the lake to find food — food like me! And there's a lone *Pterodactylus* circling the area at about 60 feet.
That's the orientation over. I guess it's time to start."

Buddy now had all the information the program was prepared to give her at this stage. She went back to her report:
"I am trying out the movement controls in my glove now. The helmet is very sensitive. When I move my head, the screen changes as it tracks my vision. I can see I'm really in the open here and I'm a bit worried about Ornitho. He's got good eyesight and a good sense of smell. I'll move toward that fern area and get my bearings. The shadow of that *Pterodactylus* just passed over. I think I'd better make a run for it — too late, it's spotted me."

The *Pterodactylus* swooped down toward the *Microvenator*. A *Pterodactylus* would not normally attack this medium-sized dinosaur, but then the *Microvenator* normally stayed in the safety of a family group. It was unusual to find a solitary *Microvenator* out of cover in broad daylight. The *Pterodactylus* had been programmed to take advantage of the *Microvenator* being on its own and then there was the Random Factor.

Buddy had no time to consider why the *Pterodactylus* was attacking. She veered left and began zigzagging and jumping. The screen flashed red, and the landscape tumbled over itself as she rolled out of control. Buddy's biodata told her she had been "wounded" and was losing blood. The chart told her that her energy level from this attack had been halved. She needed rest and food to build up her strength before the next challenge. She continued with her verbal report:
"I'm injured. I'm making for the ferns before that horrible pterosaur

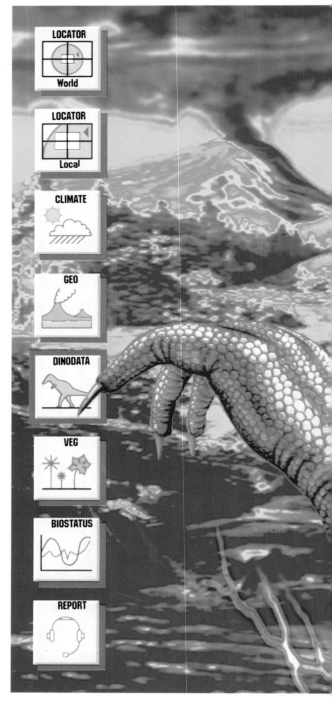

"Too late,
it's spotted me."

ALERT

Year
70 MY

U. Time
06.28

EXIT

RANDOM
EFFECT

DINODATA

PETRODACTYLUS
Wingspan: 2 ft
5 in. (75 cm)
Wing-fingered;
pointed teeth;
long, flexible neck.

ENERGY

has another go at me. In the ferns, at last. All kinds of insects in here. Enormous cockroaches and dragonflies and strange blue flying beetles. Tried eating the ferns but the plant data says they are poisonous. I need meat, but I won't be able to hunt for long with this injury draining my energy. There's a loud humming noise coming from straight ahead, like a swarm of giant mosquitoes. Moving forward ... eughhh! It's horrible, a dead something, and it's covered with thousands of beetles. Is this what I'm supposed to eat? I can't — it's disgusting. But I suppose I have to 'in the name of science'."

The Pterodactylus swooped down toward the *Microventator*.

Using the highly sensitive finger controls in her glove, Buddy clawed away at the carnivorous beetles that had crawled into the dead *Sauropelta*, and tore at the flesh with her teeth. Her energy level gradually improved from level 3 to level 6. She now needed to rest before seeking out the deinonychosaurs. But a deafening roar and the sound of crashing undergrowth changed her plans. She swiveled her head around in time to see a swift-moving, predatory *Ornithomimus* lunging toward her. She jumped sideways as the theropod's toothless jaws snapped onto part of the carcass and lifted it out of view.

Ornithomimus

"That was close," Buddy gasped. "Fortunately, I think Ornitho prefers dead meat to me at the moment. According to the locator maps, this fern swamp extends about a mile to the west. I'll move through slowly and try to pick up some more energy credits. I've noticed little pools of water — dew, I suppose — in the center of the fern leaves. Sipping these has pushed up my energy to level 8. Wait! There are some weird noises coming from up ahead. The noises are getting louder. Much louder! And I can feel the ground shaking!"

As Buddy broke out of the fern swamp she saw the most amazing sight: a herd of 30 or more *Tenontosaurus* in full stampede. They moved quickly, keeping the juveniles, who whistled like boiling kettles, protected on all sides. Buddy tried peering through the dust to see what had caused the stampede, and then she saw a *Deinonychus* running very fast on the outside of the group. This outrider was making the stampeding herd veer away from the fern swamp, and turn toward a narrow gap between huge rocks. Then Buddy realized what was happening. Two *Deinonychus* were steering the herd into an ambush! Suddenly, from behind the rocks five more *Deinonychus* appeared right in the path of the herd, which then panicked and split in two. One half raced between the gap in the rocks, the other half doubled back on itself and came to a confused halt. The predators then struck — swiftly, brutally, and with devastating efficiency. Springing four or five yards, three of them hit a dazed *Tenontosaurus*. The cruel claws raked through the animal's flesh and brought it writhing and kicking to the ground. The two outriders then fell upon its neck and killed it instantly, while the other dinosaurs in the pack feasted upon its side.

Deinonychus

Buddy knew that the more observations she made, the more credits she won for her next Dinoventure. But this was too horrible. Suddenly, a shrill piping sound made her look down. There was a young *Tenontosaurus*, detached from the herd. The clock read 8:20, which meant she had only a few minutes left in DINO. She brought her BIOSTATUS up onscreen.

DINODATA

GEO

Buddy was aware of the loss of credits as she brought back the previous screen. Something had changed. The baby dinosaur's whistling had attracted the attention of one of the *Deinonychus*. It began to walk toward them with slow deliberate strides. The baby *Tenontosaurus* suddenly went very still, as though sensing the danger. Buddy quickly weighed her options: she could try and distract the *Deinonychus*, but she could lose all her credits if "killed." Or she could EXIT early and lose another credit, but sacrifice the baby Tenonto. She made her decision, and began to move her fingers very gently in the control glove.

The control glove

"*Deinonychus*," she said out loud. "You are now going to see what a smart *Microvenator* can do. I'm moving now, and old grisly chops has seen me. He's about 100 feet away, and closing in fast. I'm running toward him. Come on you brute ... I'm jumping now ... I did it, I jumped right over him ... oh no! Right into the path of Ornitho! I can't believe it, he's ignored me. But he's frightened off the *Deinonychus*. I must find little Tenonto ..."

The screen briefly showed her status report again. Then it flickered and went blank. The game was over.

Rob helped her out of the harness. He and his father had been watching Buddy's Dinoventure on the monitor. "I only lost two credits," she said.

"And a baby *Tenontosaurus*," Rob added. Dr. Harlow came to her defense. "What you did was very brave, and I daresay dinosaurs may have made sacrifices to protect their young, though it would have been unlikely for one to risk its life for another species."

"What about baby Tenonto?" Buddy asked.

"When you exited from DINO, all the data was saved. That means the baby *Tenontosaurus* will still be there when you go back in. However, next time, Rob, it's your turn." Dr. Harlow then entered something on the computer. "Just having a look at what Rob's mission will be." He pulled down the onscreen menu. "This should be fascinating," he said chuckling. "Absolutely fascinating."

LOCATOR

Local

DINODATA

REPORT

GLOSSARY

Ankylosaur ("stiff reptile"): An armored dinosaur, with bony plates covering much of the body, tail, neck, and head. A group that existed in the Jurassic and Cretaceous periods.

Badlands: Open lands, particularly in North America, where there are very few plants. The land surface erodes rapidly because rainfall can wash away soil and surface rock. Normally, plants stop this. Badlands may contain deep valleys and high rock pinnacles.

Butte: A tall, straight-sided mass of rock in a badlands area that has been eroded all around by wind and rain. The butte may have escaped erosion because it has a cap of hard rock that was not worn away.

Continent: A major land mass, such as Africa, Europe, or North America.

Cretaceous ("of the chalk"): The third and final period of the "Age of Dinosaurs"—from 145 to 65 million years ago.

Deinonychosaur ("fearful claw reptile"): A meat-eating dinosaur, belonging to a group of active hunters that are best known in the Cretaceous. Typical members include *Deinonychus* and *Velociraptor*.

Erosion: The wearing away of rocks and soil by wind, rain, rivers, and the sea.

Evolution ("unrolling"): The way in which plants and animals have changed through time.

Extinction ("disappearing"): The dying out of a group of plants or animals.

Food Chain: The normal passage of food through living communities. The chain begins with plants, which are eaten by plant-eating animals. The plant eaters are then eaten by meat eaters, and these in turn may be eaten by bigger meat eaters. In the end, the dead bodies of animals break down and are eaten by microbes. They then form food for the plants.

Jurassic ("from the Jura Mountains"): The second part or middle period of the "Age of the Dinosaurs"—from 205 to 145 million years ago.

Mammal ("suckling animal"): A warm-blooded, backboned animal, covered in hair, and feeding its young with milk; mice, bats, cats, dolphins, horses, and humans are all mammals.

Mesozoic ("middle life"): The whole of the "Age of the Dinosaurs," consisting of the Triassic, Jurassic, and Cretaceous periods. It lasted from 245 to 65 million years ago.

Muscle: A strong, fibrous fleshy part of the body, that runs from one bone to another, and moves that part of the body.

Nocturnal: Animals that feed and move around at night.

Predator: A meat eater, and animal that preys on other animals.

Protein: The basic chemical units that make up plants and animals.

Pterosaur ("wing reptile"): Ancient flying reptile with wings of skin rather than feathers. Not a dinosaur.

Reptile ("creeping one"): A scaled, cold-blooded, backboned animal, such as a turtle, lizard, snake, crocodile, or dinosaur.

Sauropod ("reptile foot"): Large, four-legged plant eater with a long neck and long tail. Member of a group of dinosaurs that lived in Jurassic and Cretaceous times.

Subtropical: Areas of the world that lie just north and south of the tropics.

Theropod ("beast foot"): Meat-eating dinosaur. The theropods include all meat-eating dinosaurs.

Triassic ("three-part"): The first part of the "Age of the Dinosaurs"—from 245 to 205 million years ago.

Tropical: Areas of the world that lie around the equator.

INDEX

Page numbers in *italic* refer to the illustrations

KINGFISHER
Larousse Kingfisher Chambers Inc.
95 Madison Avenue
New York, New York 10016

First American edition 1994
2 4 6 8 10 9 7 5 3 1

Library of Congress Cataloging-in-Publication Data
Benton, Michael.
Deinonychus / by Michael Benton. — 1st American ed.
p.   cm. — (Dinoworld)
Includes index.
1. Deinonychus—Juvenile literature.   [1. Deinonychus.
2. Dinosaurs.)   I. Title. II. Series.
QE862.S3B44   1994
567.9'7—dc20   93–43402 CIP AC

ISBN 1–85697–991–1

Series Editor: Michèle Byam
Series Designer: Shaun Barlow
Picture Research: Elaine Willis

Dinoventures are written
by Jim Miles

Additional help from Andy Archer, Cathy Tincknell,
Matthew Gore, Smiljka Surla, and Hilary Bird

The publishers wish to thank the following artists for
contributing to the book:
Marion Appleton, Richard Bonson, Adrian Chesterman
(The Art Collection), Barry Croucher (Wildlife Artists Agency), Eugene
Fleury, Terry Gabby (Eva Morris AFA), Peter Gudynas, Terence Lambert,
Adrian Lascomb (Garden Studios), Roger Payne
(Linden Artists), Justine Peak, Andrew Robinson
(Garden Studios), Studio Boni Lalli, David Wright
(Kathy Jakeman)

The publishers wish to thank the following for
supplying photographs for the book:
The Natural History Museum, London; Yale Peabody
Museum of Natural History

Printed in Spain